A Yummy Lunch

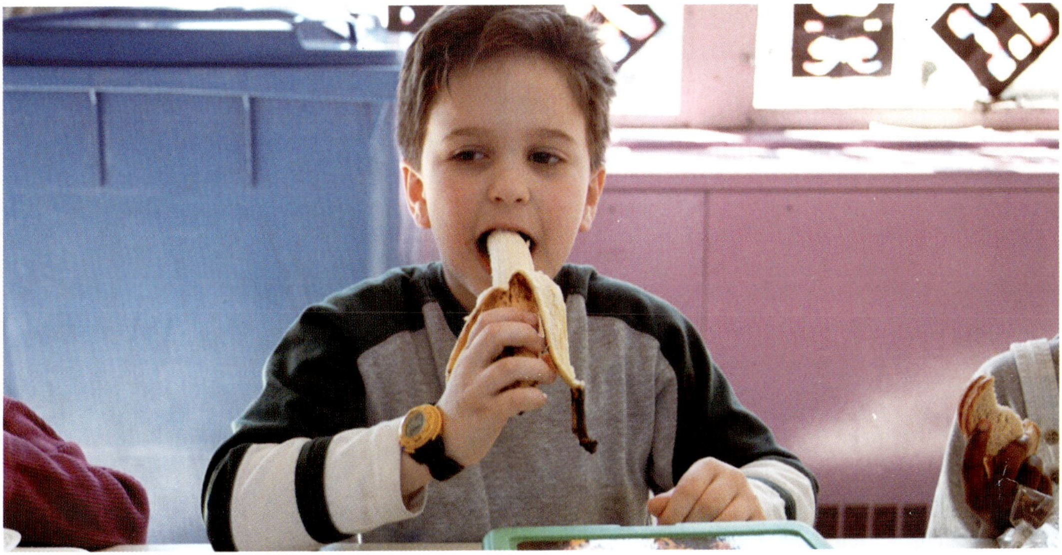

by
Michèle Dufresne

Pioneer Valley Educational Press, Inc.

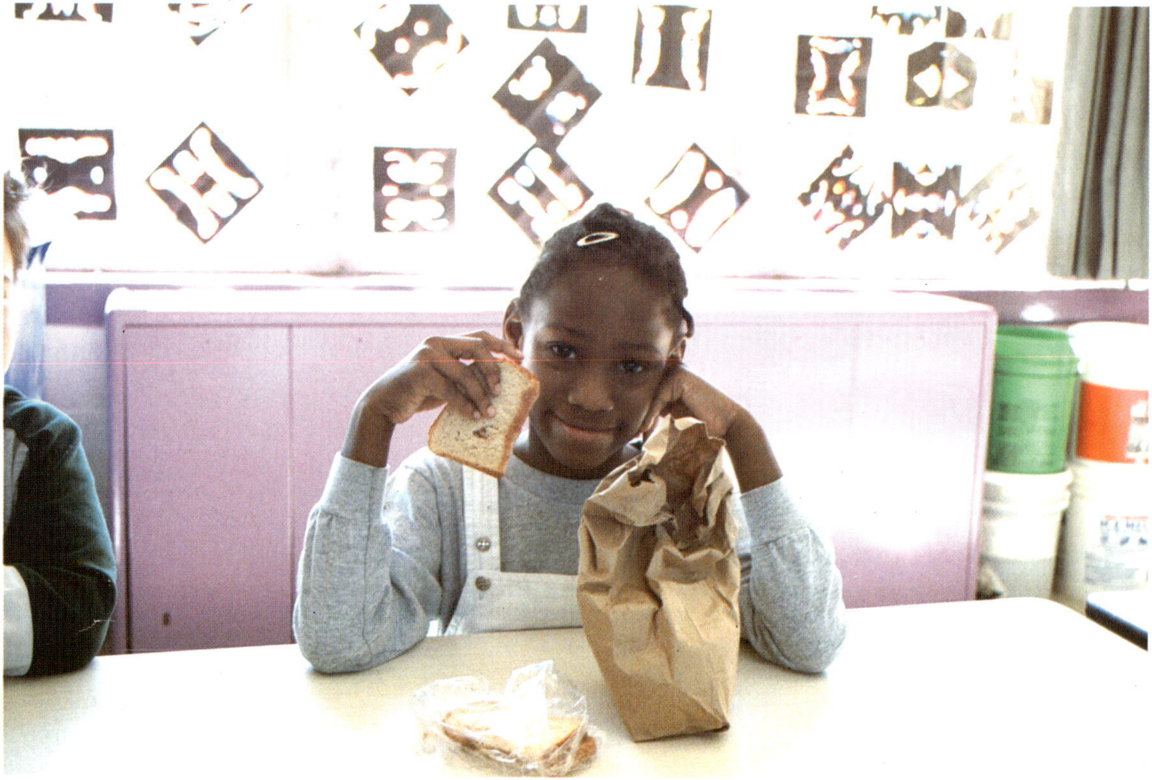

Here is a sandwich.

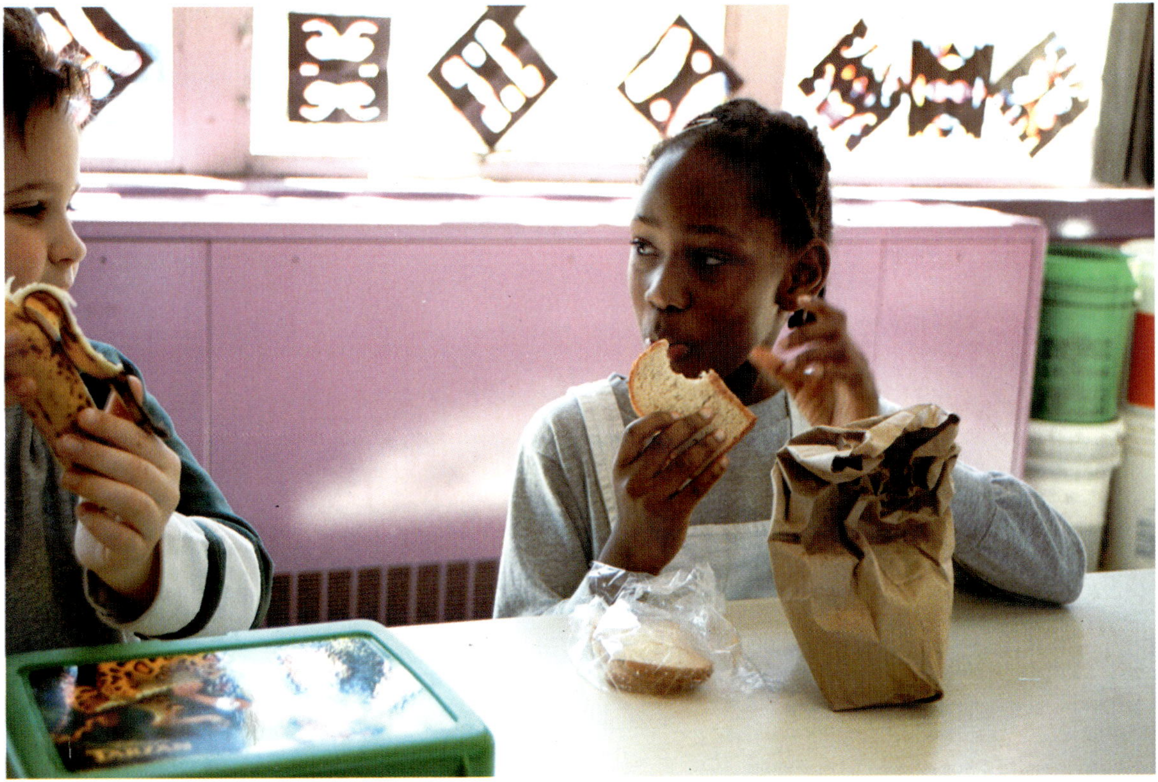

Yum!

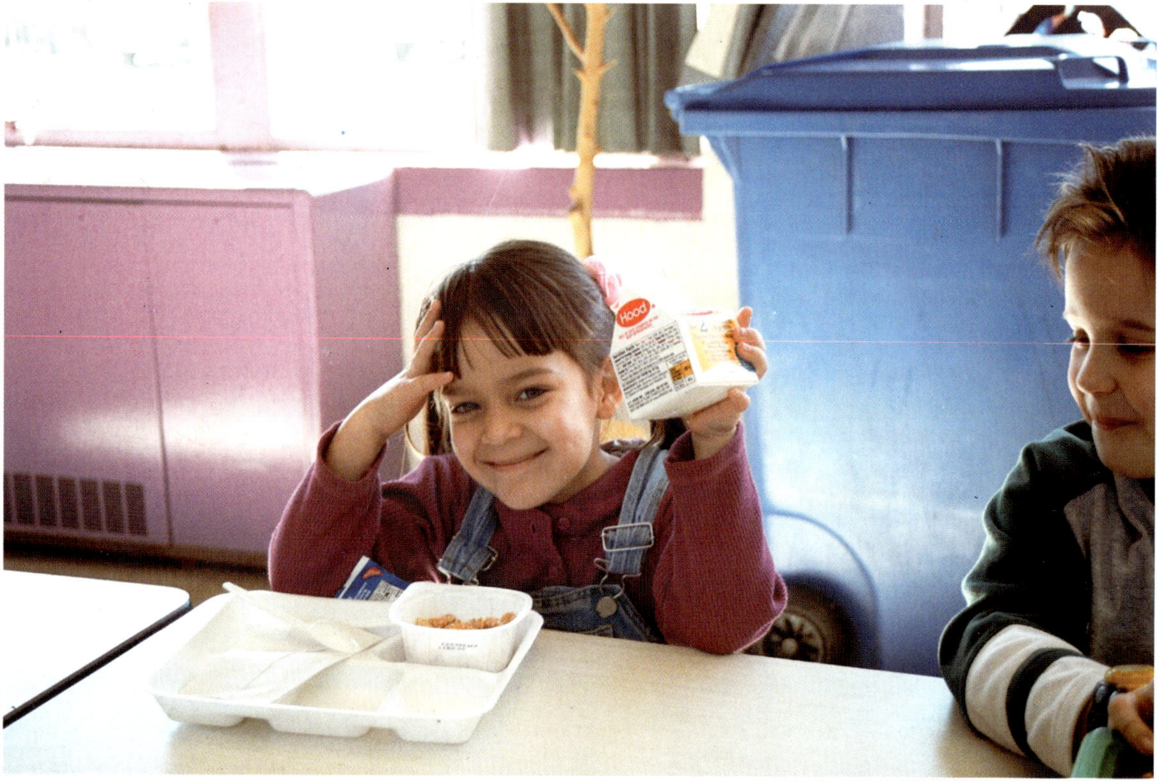

Here is milk.

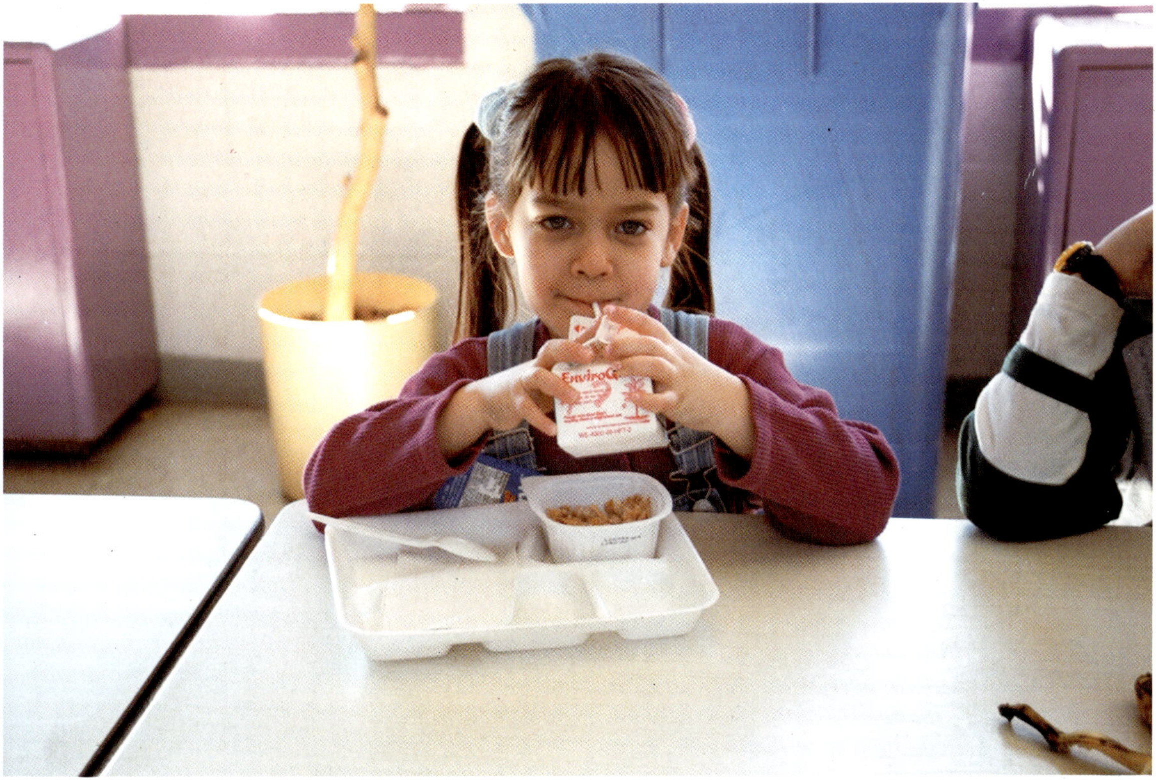

Yum, yum!

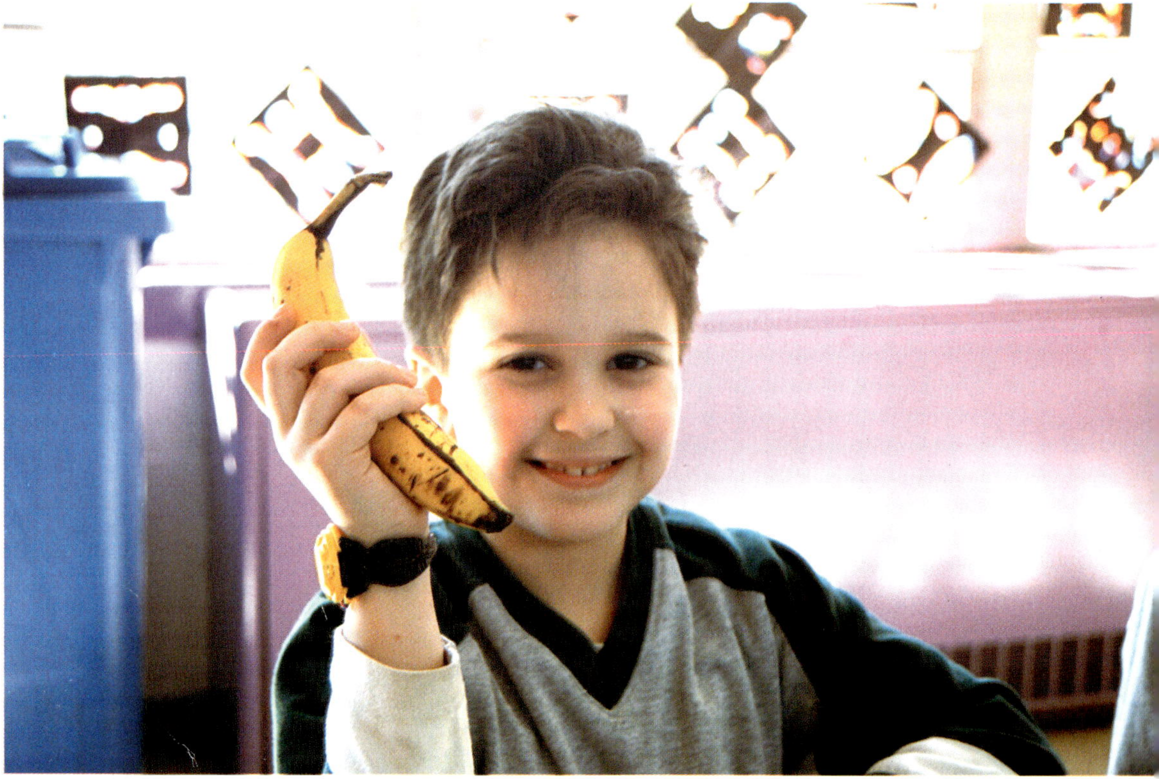

Here is a banana.

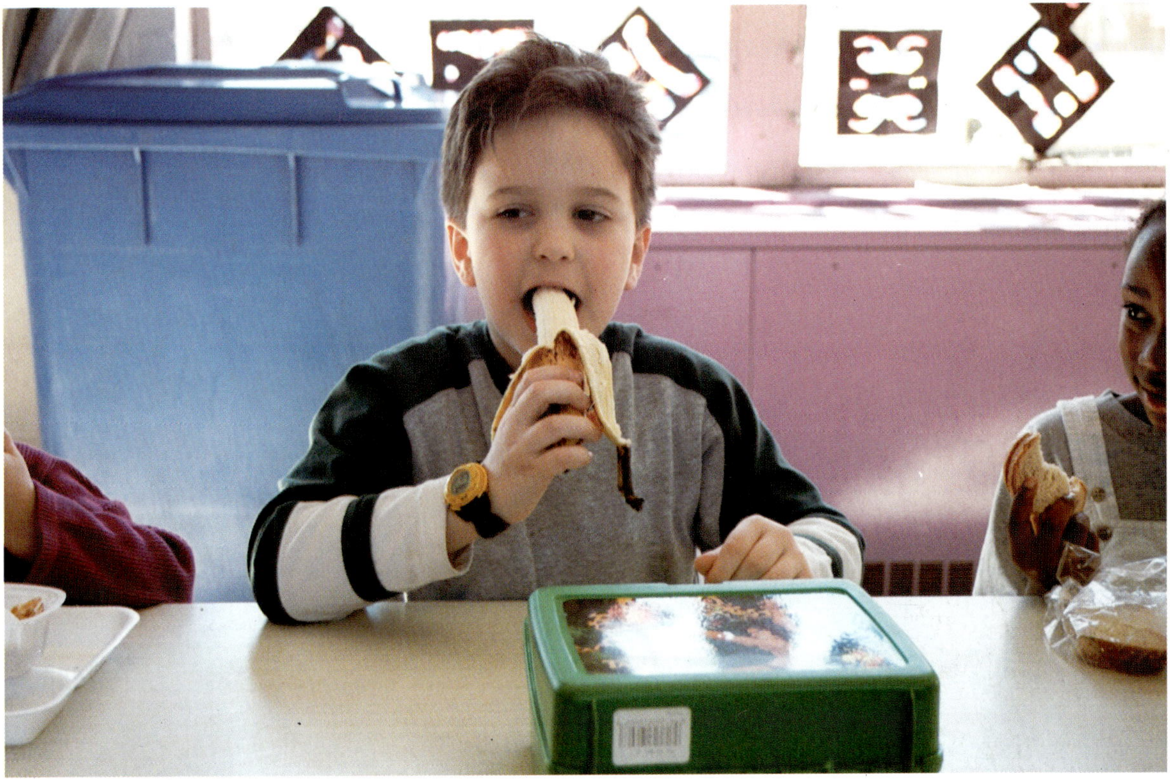

Yum!

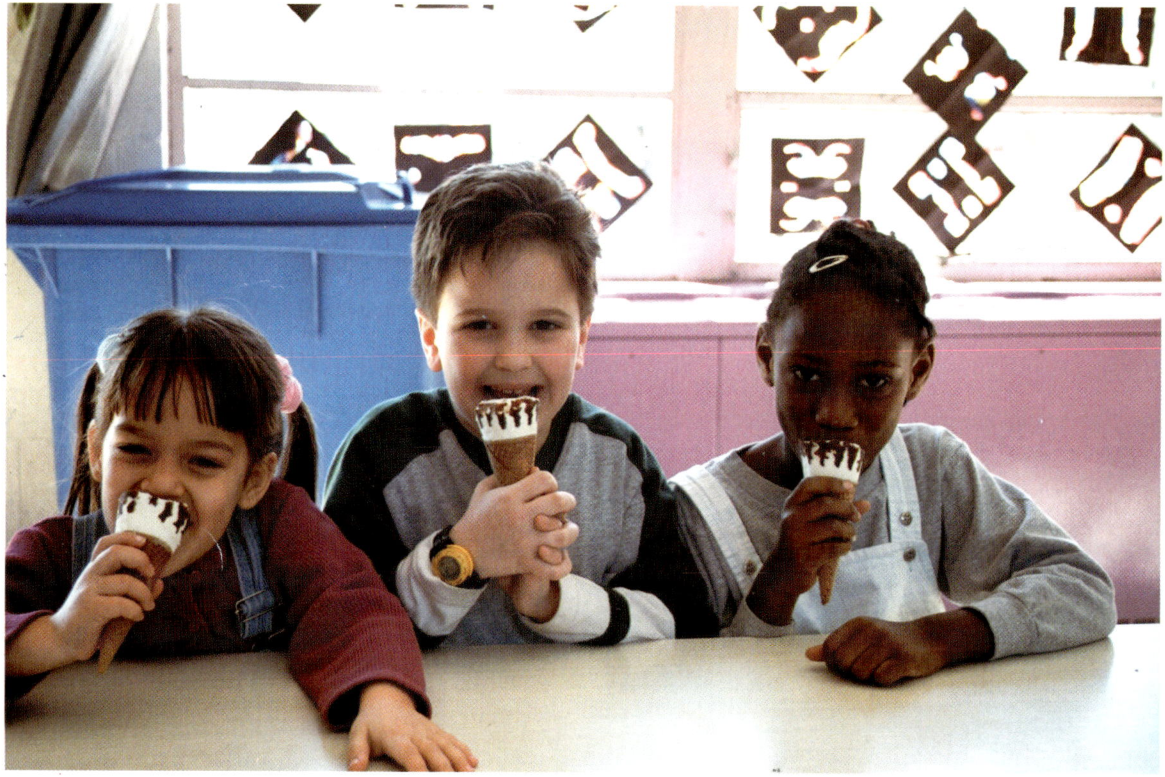

Here is ice cream.
Yum, yum, yum!